Jeanette Walls

The Glass Castle

BookCaps™ Study Guide
<u>www.bookcaps.com</u>

© 2012. All Rights Reserved.

Table of Contents

Historical Background

The Glass Castle by Jeannette Walls is a memoir that tells the story of Wall's unique childhood growing up with two eccentric parents who in their search for adventure often failed to provide for basics such as dinner for their children. Walls's husband encouraged the writing of her memoir by convincing her that everyone appealing has a past. Her engaging storytelling style is influenced by her experience as a journalist.

Walls's reporter instincts also made her want to tell her story in the most honest way that she could; she chose to include even the details that were embarrassing or difficult to share about her family. Walls is married to the writer John Taylor and currently lives in Virginia and New York. She is a regular contributing reporter to MSNBC.com and has published a novel called *Half Broke Horses*. *The Glass Castle* was the winner of a Christopher Award and spent nearly three years on the New York Times bestseller list.

Plot Summary

Told in 5 parts, *The Glass Castle* documents Jeannette Walls's tumultuous childhood moving from place to place in the Southwest and then facing challenges in Welch, West Virginia. The memoir begins with Jeannette as an adult living in New York City. Jeannette is in a taxi on the way to a party when she sees her mother digging through a dumpster on the side of the road. Too embarrassed to say hello, Jeannette has her driver take her back to her Park Avenue apartment.

Part II backtracks to Jeannette's earliest memory—getting severe burns while boiling hot dogs by herself at the age of three. Jeannette was in the hospital for six weeks but was soon back to boiling hot dogs and playing with fire. A few months later Jeannette's father came home in the middle of the night and told the family it was time to do the skedaddle. Together with her parents, older sister Lori, and younger brother Brian, Jeannette hopped in the car and moved. Her family was always moving from place to place, stopping in various locations such as Las Vegas and San Francisco. But the family usually ended up in small mining towns where Rex would get jobs as an electrician but spend most of the income on cigarettes, alcohol, and gambling.

The two places where the Walls family spent the most time were Battle Mountain and Phoenix. In Battle Mountain Rex tried to strike it rich by finding gold and told his children that when he had enough money he would build them an incredible house he named the Glass Castle. Jeannette's mother Rose Mary gave birth to another child whom she named Maureen after weeks of debate. When the family moved to Phoenix they lived in a home Rose Mary had inherited from her mother. Jeannette had various escapades there including petting a cheetah at the zoo, riding her bicycle all over town, and narrowly avoiding the neighborhood pedophiles. However, money was sometimes so tight that the family went hungry, and Rex's alcoholism got so miserable that he got into dangerous and destructive fights with Rose Mary.

Eventually money got so tight that the family moved to Welch, West Virginia to live with Rex's parents for a while. Jeannette's grandmother Erma was a mean alcoholic who at one point attempted to molest Brian. Tensions got so high that Rex and Rose Mary bought a dilapidated house on Little Hobart Street that lacked indoor plumbing. The family was dirt poor and the children often fought with other kids. They stayed in Welch for years, in which Jeannette developed a passion for journalism and had various adventures and mishaps. Rex continued in a downward spiral of alcoholism and Rose Mary often refused to go to her job.

When Lori graduated high school she left Welch for New York City. The rest of the children followed in Lori's footsteps in the following years. Eventually Rex and Rose Mary came along too although they soon found themselves homeless while their children prospered. Jeannette got a degree from Barnard College and started a career as a journalist. Lori and Brian were equally successful. Meanwhile, Rex and Rose Mary continued in their old ways. Maureen was arrested for stabbing Rose Mary and sent to a mental health hospital for a year. Rex died of a heart attack at the age of 59. Years later the family got together and remembered the craziness of the years they spent together.

Themes

Life on the Move

Jeannette spends the early years of her childhood
moving around so much that it's hard for her to keep
track of all the places she's lived. Her family would
leave town in the middle of the night, often with no
warning, to "do the skedaddle" as Jeannette's dad
called it. Sometimes Rex moved the family because
he lost a job and things got too tight, but more often
the moves were motivated by his sense of adventure
and yearning for somewhere new. As the memoir
documents, life on the move can indeed be an
adventure, but living without roots can also be
difficult and isolating.

Alcoholism

As the memoir progresses, it becomes clear that Rex's frequent drinking binges are signs of a greater addiction. Although Rex is normally funny and inventive, when he drinks he becomes destructive and a hazard to his family. Rex's alcoholism becomes so serious that, for one birthday, Jeannette tells her father that all she wants is for him to quit drinking. Rex lasts the summer but then returns to the bottle. As his life becomes more dependent on liquor, Rex begins to steal money from his wife and children that they desperately need to put food on the table. *The Glass Castle*'s honest depiction of how Rex's struggles affected the entire family shows the devastating effect alcoholism can have on family life.

Remaining a Family

Jeannette's parents tell her to forget what anyone else thinks of her because her family is all that matters. The family is the central unit in *The Glass Castle*, the one constant among an everchanging setting and cast of characters. As Jeannette and her siblings grow into teenagers and young adults, they begin to leave Welch, West Virginia to follow their own dreams. Even then, the siblings remain together and all move to New York City, where their parents eventually follow them. *The Glass Castle* shows that, despite all the hardships and dysfunctions, a family will always remain a family—for better or for worse.

Self-Sufficiency

Jeannette's mother is a whopping advocate for self-sufficiency, and she tries to instill this same sense of independence in her children. Rose Mary Walls is never bothered when her children go off on their own or make stupid mistakes because she claims it is the only way they will learn. She is also a staunch critic of welfare, claiming that being poor is something that a person can overcome, but once you're on welfare, you're a charity case forever. Although her views are extreme, Rose Mary sticks to her opinions even when she is living on the streets of New York. Her dedication is something that both inspires and frustrates Jeannette.

Tough Love

As Jeannette Walls realizes from a young age, love can sometimes be difficult and exhausting, especially when as a child you take on more responsibilities than your parents just to get by. At various points in her childhood, Jeannette had to use "tough love" by saying things that were painful to hear but honest and well intentioned. One such time was when Jeannette told her father that all she wanted for her birthday was for him to stop drinking. Another was when she pushed her mother to keep a teaching job even though it made her mom unhappy. *The Glass Castle* shows the importance of helping your loved ones, even when it's hard.

Dreaming Big

Rex Walls, for all his shortcomings, is a man who likes to think out of the box and dream big. Despite his alcoholism and low-paying jobs, Rex never loses faith that he will strike it rich by finding gold in California or else by inventing a new coal mining technology. Rex's grandiose dreams are epitomized by his plans to build the glass castle, for which the memoir is named. The glass castle is a large house made of glass that will rely on solar technology. Rex tells his children on multiple occasions that he will build the house for them. Although the plans never come to fruition, Rex never lets go of his imagination and hopes for the future.

Forgiving Shortcomings

Jeannette's family is far from perfect. In fact, it is usually veering on the edge of dysfunctional. Despite this, Jeannette never gives up on them altogether and always forgives and moves forward. Jeannette's forgiveness is particularly evident in her relationship with her father Rex. When Rex wants something, he always asks Jeannette if he has ever let her down. Although he has indeed let her down on too many occasions to count, Jeannette still can never bare to answer that question with anything other than yes. Her soft spot for her father despite his many flaws illustrates that while she does not always approve of her parents' choices, she will always love them.

Facing Fears

Jeannette's first memory is of her shirt catching fire while she cooked hot dogs alone at the age of three. The burns on her abdomen were so severe that she was hospitalized for six weeks and received permanent scars. Despite this, soon after Jeannette returned home she started cooking hot dogs again, and her father taught her how to flick her finger through a flame so it doesn't burn. Jeannette's newfound fascination with fire and refusal to back down from the force that had hurt her is indicative of a greater theme throughout the memoir of facing fears. Every member of the Walls family has his or her own demons to fight, and all show in their own way that courage is one of the most fundamental values a person can have.

Parental Responsibility

Parental responsibility, or lack thereof, is a constant theme throughout the memoir. For better or worse, the Walls parents let their children run around unsupervised, make their own decisions, and fend for themselves. While this parenting tactic taught Jeannette and her siblings to be self-sufficient and not make the same mistakes twice, it also meant that they had singularly little guidance or protection from negative influences in the world: alcoholism, financial irresponsibility, hunger, and even child abuse. *The Glass Castle* does not make any definitive statements about the responsibilities a parent has to a child, but it does question how one's past and childhood affects one's outlook on life.

Poverty

All throughout Jeannette's childhood, Jeannette's parents barely scraped by and never quite mastered effectively holding a budget. Jeannette rarely had proper clothes, only bathed occasionally, and sometimes ate popcorn for days on end because there was no food in the house. The poverty in Jeannette's family was sometimes due to chance and poor luck, but just as often it was due to her father's drinking and gambling and her mother's unwillingness to hold a steady job or sell off her land or jewelry. Jeannette's personal experience shows that poverty can often have a complicated set of causes but always has difficult results.

Characters

Jeannette Walls

The author of the memoir, Jeannette bravely shares the story of her childhood, leaving nothing back in the exploration of her past. As a child, Jeannette is loving but practical, at odds with peers, and an aspiring journalist who vows to live differently than her parents.

Rex Walls

Jeannette's father, Rex is charismatic, intelligent, and always thinking out of the box. When he drinks, however, Rex can be impulsive, irresponsible, and even dangerous. Rex shares a peculiar bond with Jeanette, whom he calls Mountain Goat and considers his biggest fan.

Rose Mary Walls

Jeannette's mother, Rose Mary is an artist and a certified teacher. She is a free spirit and encourages all the Walls children to be self-sufficient and figure out how to look after themselves.

Brian Walls

Jeannette's younger brother by one year, Brian is the closest to Jeannette in age and personality. He goes on various adventures with Jeannette in their childhood and eventually follows her to New York where he becomes a police officer.

Lori Walls

Jeannette's older sister, Lori is considered the "brilliant one" of the family. She is an aspiring artist and is the first of the Walls children to leave Welch, West Virginia for New York City.

Maureen Walls

Jeannette's younger sister, Maureen has blonde hair and blue eyes and is considered the "pretty one" of the family. She eventually develops mental health issues and stabs Jeannette's mother after a bad fight.

Billy Deel

A boy who moves to Battle Mountain when Jeannette is eight. He is a juvenile delinquent who takes a liking to Jeannette and then harasses her in a tool shed while they are playing hide-and-seek.

Erma Walls

Rex's mother, Erma is an alcoholic and West Virginia native. She dislikes her grandchildren and relegates them to the basement after Jeannette accuses her of touching Brian inappropriately.

Dinitia Hewitt

A black girl in Welch who first bullies Jeannette but later befriends her. She invites Jeannette to swim with her one morning, but their friendship never fully develops because of outside racial pressures at the time

Jeanette Bivens

An English teacher in Welch who encourages Jeannette to be a journalist for the school paper. She was Rex's teacher as well, and he named Jeannette after her because she was the only teacher to ever believe in him.

Chapter Summaries

Part I- A Woman on the Street

The Glass Castle begins in New York City when Jeannette Walls looks out the window of her taxi to see her mother standing fifteen feet away, picking out food from a dumpster. Jeannette has not seen her mother in months, but she can tell her mom's mannerisms immediately despite the fact that her hair is tangled and her clothes ratty and worn down. Rather than say hello, Jeannette tells her taxi driver to turn around and drive her back to her apartment.

Jeannette walks by her doorman and goes up the stairs to her apartment on Park Avenue. She looks around her apartment—a space she has worked hard to decorate and turn into a home—and is overwhelmed with guilt that she has so much while her parents are living on the street. But she reasons to herself that there is little she can do. Whenever she asks her mom if she needs anything, she asks for something trivial like a perfume atomizer. Jeannette's parents are living the lifestyle they want to be living.

Jeannette calls a friend of her mother's and leaves a message. This is her way of getting in touch with her mom, who usually calls back from a payphone a few days later. When Jeannette next hears from her mom they agree to go out for dinner. At the Chinese restaurant where they meet up, Jeannette mentions having seen her mom from the taxi and says that she is worried. Jeannette's mom says she's fine and asks why Jeannette didn't say hi from the taxi. When Jeannette admits she was too ashamed to acknowledge she knew the crazy-looking woman on the street, her mother points her chopsticks and says that Jeannette is the one who needs help because her values are all confused. Jeannette sighs and what she's supposed to do when people ask about her parents. Her mom says just to tell the honest truth.

Part II- The Desert (Sections 1-4)

Jeannette's earliest memory is of her clothes catching
fire as she boiled hot dogs over a stove at age three.
She was alone in the kitchen as she felt the flames
leap up toward her face. She screamed. Jeannette's
mother came running and wrapped her in an army
surplus blanket to put out the flames. She drove
Jeannette to the hospital in a borrowed car from the
woman who lived in the trailer next door. Jeannette's
burns were so severe that she received multiple skin
grafts and stayed in the hospital for six weeks.

During her time in the hospital, the nurses and doctors asks Jeannette all sorts of questions about home and if anyone had ever mistreated her. She insisted that no one had ever hurt her; she just cooked alone because her mother thought she was mature for her age. Jeannette liked being in the hospital because the nurses were always asking how she was feeling, and everything was shiny and new inside. Jeannette's father Rex argued with the doctors over Jeannette's bandages—the doctors said she needed them to prevent infection, but her dad said to hell with infection, burns needed to breathe so they wouldn't scar. When Jeannette had been in the hospital for about six months, her dad came to visit alone and told her they were going to check out Rex Walls-style. He picked Jeannette up and ran down the hospital halls with nurses yelling after him. They jumped into the car Jeannette's mother had been idling in the parking lot and sped away.

Several days later, Jeannette began cooking hot dogs alone again. Her mother approved of this decision, insisting that Jeannette couldn't live in fear of something as basic as fire. The burns had the opposite effect—Jeannette became fascinated with flames and started stealing her father's cigarette matches to play. In one such experiment, she accidently melted off the face of her favorite Tinker Bell doll.

A few months later Rex woke the whole family in the middle of the night to announce that they were leaving town. Whenever the family picked up and moved like this, Rex called it doing the skedaddle. Jeannette cried when Rex threw their cat Quixote to the curb, but her mother told her not to be so sentimental—Quixote was going to be a wild cat now, which was more fun than being a house cat anyway.

Whenever the family did the skedaddle, Rex would make up an elaborate story about how the FBI was after them. However, Jeannette's mom Rose Mary told the kids that the feds weren't thoroughly after them; their father just thought it sounded more exciting than bill collectors. The family moved like nomads through countless mining towns in the Southwest. Sometimes they stopped at Jeannette's Grandma Smith's house. Sometimes they enrolled in school in the towns the stayed in, but not always. Rex claimed that their constant moving was all to find gold. He invented a contraption called the Prospector that would sift through dirt to find gold deposits.

When inventing or telling stories, Rex was telling his kids Lori, Jeannette, and Brian about his plans for building the Glass Castle. Rex planned to use all his engineering skills to construct a giant house in the desert that would have everything from a glass ceiling to a glass staircase. It would use solar energy for its central heating and even have its own water purification system. Once the Walls family struck rich with the Prospector, they would finally have their Glass Castle.

Part II- The Desert (Sections 5-11)

One day when Jeannette was four and Lori seven, the two sisters tried to count how many places they had lived. They got up to eleven but then lost track. They were at a rest stop on the way to Las Vegas. When the car started moving again, Rex took a sharp turn and the door flew open. Jeannette went tumbling out of the car and scraped up her head and elbows in the fall. The car sped along without her, and Jeannette started to cry by the railroad tracks where she had fallen, thinking that her family was deserting her like they had done with Quixote the cat. The car did come back eventually, and Rex promised he would never leave her behind.

They lived in Las Vegas for about a month while Rex tried to make it rich gambling. Next they moved to a cheap hotel in San Francisco. One night there was a fire in the hotel room. Jeannette couldn't help but wonder if the fire was out to get her. After the hotel burned down, the family lived on the beach for a few days and then Rex decided it was time to move back to the desert, claiming that cities will kill you. They rented a house in a small town called Midland. One night in Midland Jeannette thought there was a creature in the room with her so Rex took her Demon Hunting in the desert. His nickname for Jeannette was Mountain Goat because she never fell when they were climbing mountains.

Jeannette and her siblings never believed in Santa Claus or received much by way of Christmas presents. The Christmas they spent in Midland Rex took the three kids outside one by one and told them to pick a star that would be their present. Jeannette picked Venus, which was a planet, but her father let her have it all the same. By this point, Rose Mary was pregnant again. The family hit the road to reach a bigger city where Rose Mary could give birth. On the way, Rex and Rose Mary got into a fight over how long Rose Mary had been pregnant. Rose Mary claimed she was 10 months pregnant, and Rex thought that was nonsense. Rex had been drinking, and the fight soon escalated to such an extreme that Rose Mary got out of the car, and Rex tried to run her over. The next day the two made up and acted as if nothing had happened.

The big city the family moved to was called Blythe. Two months later, when Rose Mary claimed she was 12 months pregnant, she gave birth to a girl. The baby went without a name for weeks, but they eventually settled on Maureen. A few months after Maureen was born a cop tried to pull over Rex's car, but Rex sped away because he said if the cop pulled him over, he'd discover the car had no registration papers. The next day Rex decided it was time to do the skedaddle once more and the family packed up for a new adventure.

Part II- The Desert (Sections 12-19)

The family ended up in Battle Mountain, Arizona, a mining town with lots of empty sky and run-down buildings. The family moved into a wooden house on the edge of town by the railroad tracks. They improvised for furniture. Rose Mary wanted a piano so Rex found a cheap one but messed up moving it. The piano ended up in the backyard, where Rose Mary said they had the privilege of playing for the great outdoors and the neighbors too.

Rex got a job as an electrician in one of the mines. He came home early and hung out with the kids in the afternoon. When Rex wasn't around, Jeannette and her siblings created their own games to entertain themselves. Jeannette and Brian especially liked to go exploring in the desert. They would go on their own gold hunts, and Jeannette started an extensive rock collection. On Saturday night if Rex had money they would eat out at a place called Owl City. After, they would sit around the living room together, each family member reading his respective book. All were avid readers and Jeannette loved *Black Beauty* the most.

Rose Mary enrolled Lori, Jeannette, and Brian in Mary S. Black Elementary School. The classes were too easy for Jeannette since her dad had already taught her a lot of the material. None of the Walls children were given an allowance so when they wanted money they would collect bottles and scrap metals. When they saved enough they would buy candy and drive the candy storeowner crazy because they spent so long deciding what they wanted. On the way back, they passed by a house called the Green Lantern, which their mother said was a cathouse. Once Jeannette double-dared Brian to go to talk to one of the ladies who sat around on the porch of the Green Lantern. Nearly six years old and fearless, Brian obliged. When he returned he reported that the woman was not scary after all. She said the Green Lantern was a place where men visited, and the women were sympathetic to them.

One day Rex took the kids out to a local hot spring. Jeannette didn't know how to swim and was terrified, but Rex pulled her right into the middle of the lake and kept throwing her in the water. Jeannette would thrash and almost drown. She would cling to Rex only to have him throw her in again and again until eventually she learned to keep afloat herself.

Sometime later Rex lost his job at the mine. He started doing odd jobs and gambling, but money was often tight and sometimes there was little to no food around. One day there was nothing in the whole fridge but a stick of margarine. Lori claimed that if you mixed it with sugar it tasted just like frosting. It didn't, but the two girls were so hungry they didn't care. When Rose Mary found out she was furious and said she had been saving the margarine. Jeannette retorted that it was the only thing in the whole house, and they were *hungry*.

That night Rose Mary got into a big fight with Rex about his empty promises. The fight lasted ages and culminated with Rose Mary dangling from the second floor window. Rose Mary swore Rex had pushed her but Rex said Rose Mary had jumped, and he was trying to help her. The very next morning Rose Mary went to school with the kids and applied for a teaching job. She was hired and assigned to Lori's class, where she was well liked by the kids but terrible at disciplining. The financial situation didn't improve much, however, because Rex would steal the paycheck and continue to use the money on booze and gambling.

Part II-The Desert (Sections 20-27)

Just after Jeannette's eighth birthday, a boy named Billy Deel moved to Battle Mountain with his father. Billy smoked cigarettes and was a certified juvenile delinquent. He developed a crush on Jeannette and gave her a ring. She accepted it on the condition that she was his friend and not his girlfriend. One day while the neighborhood kids were playing hide-and-seek Billy squeezed into a tool shed where Jeannette was hiding even though there wasn't certainly room. He tried to kiss her and tugged at her shorts. Jeannette resisted and the other kids came running at the sounds of the struggle. The next day when Jeannette went to give back her ring, Bill shouted at her that he had raped her. Jeannette didn't know what rape meant so she looked it up in the dictionary that night.

The next day while the kids were alone in the house, Billy came by with his BB gun and started attacking them. Lori went upstairs and grabbed their father's real gun. She shot a few stray bullets to scare Billy away. Later a cop car came by with Jeannette's parents. The officer said the kids would have to go to court the next day. That night Rex said it was time to do the skedaddle again and head for Phoenix. The kids were only allowed to bring one thing so Jeannette brought her favorite geode from her rock collection. On the way to Phoenix, Rose Mary told the kids that Grandma Smith died months ago, and they were going to a house in Phoenix that Rose Mary had inherited. Jeannette was devastated her mother didn't even tell her about her own grandmother's death.

The family settled into life in Phoenix—the kids enrolled in school and took gifted classes, Rose Mary opened an art studio in their house, and Rex joined the local electricians' union. Things were better financially, and Rex bought the kids bicycles and an electric washing machine. Still, the house was cockroach and termite infested, but Jeannette's parents didn't take any serious strides to fix the problem. The family had intriguing neighbors including a Gypsy clan that all lived in one house and a handful of perverts who would try to get Jeannette and her siblings to talk to them on the way to school.

After a while, city life began to get to Rex. He yearned to be out in the desert again. Around this time, Rex lost his job and then got fired from a series of jobs after that. They did not go hungry like in Battle Mountain, but things were tight again, and the kids even helped their mother shoplift a few times. Rose Mary decided she wanted a real Christmas that year so the kids picked out real presents for everyone and they even got a cheap Christmas tree on Christmas day. But that night Rex came home so drunk that he caused a fight and lit fire to the tree, ruining the Christmas they had spent weeks planning.

That Spring Jeannette turned ten. Even though birthdays weren't a tremendous deal in the family, Rex remembered. He took Jeannette outside and told her she could have anything she wanted. Jeannette told her father she wanted him to stop drinking. Rex said she must be terribly ashamed of her old man. But the next week he began to detox. The process was awful, and Rex stayed in bed for days with delusions. He spent the summer recuperating but stayed sober. At the end of the summer, he was back to drinking again, however. With Rex unemployed, Rose Mary decided it was time to go to West Virginia and stay with his parents.

Part III- Welch (Sections 28-36)

The Walls family drove from Phoenix, Arizona to Welch, West Virginia in a beat up car Rose Mary had purchased through a radio special. The journey took almost a whole month. When they finally reached Welch, they went to Rex's parents' house. It was the first time Jeannette had ever met her paternal grandparents—Erma and Ted. Jeannette's Uncle Stanley also lived in the house. Erma was a mean-spirited woman who drank too much and took an instant dislike to the children. The family moved into the basement for some time while Rex looked for work.

Jeannette and Brian enrolled in Welch Elementary. They couldn't understand the principal's accent so she assumed they had needs. The kids were unwelcoming and three black girls were particularly cruel to Jeannette, beating her up daily during recess. The ringleader of the bullies was a girl named Dinitia Hewitt. The bullying continued for weeks until one day Jeannette rescued a younger boy from a dog and walked him home. The boy ended up being Dinitia's neighbor, and from the porch across the street Dinitia observed what Jeannette had done. From then on Dinitia let up her bullying and even asked Jeannette for help with homework. Jeannette figured this was as close as she would ever get to an apology and accepted. When Erma heard about this, she made some racist comments that upset Jeannette.

In late winter Rex and Rose Mary decided to take a solo trip back to Phoenix to collect some of the stuff they had left behind in the house. The kids were left alone with Erma, who continued to be irritable and unwelcoming. One day Erma noticed a rip in Brian's pants and told him it would be easiest to mend if he kept the pants on while she sewed. Jeannette followed them into the bedroom and saw Erma grabbing at Brian's crotch while he cried. Jeannette accused Erma of being a pervert and Lori ended up hitting Erma. Erma was so angry that she made the kids stay only in the basement until their parents came back. When Rex and Rose Mary returned from Phoenix they were furious at all of the kids for disrespecting their grandmother. Rex acted particularly weird, and the kids wondered if maybe Erma used to touch her own father like that.

Since there was so much tension in Erma's house, the family moved to their own place in a poor part of town. 93 Little Hobart Street was a run-down house that didn't even have indoor plumbing. Rex told the kids that the house was only temporary—he intended to finally build the Glass Castle on the plot of land. Brian and Jeannette dug a gigantic hole in the backyard for the foundation of the Glass Castle but then Rex started using the hole to dump the family's garbage. It became increasingly clear that he would never build the house and also that Rex was not planning on doing the skedaddle anytime soon. Jeannette tried to make 93 Little Hobart Street into more of a home, but no one else in the family seemed to think it was worth the effort. On one occasion, Jeannette spent all day painting the house a bright yellow but she couldn't reach all the way so the house remained permanently half-painted.

When things got tight, Jeannette's mother reminded her that other families on Little Hobart Street had it worse. One such family was the Pastors. The mother, Ginnie Sue Pastor, was considered the town whore. Each of her children was rumored to have a different father. The Walls children fought a lot in Welch, waging mini wars on enemies that gave them a hard time. One of Jeannette and Brian's biggest triumphs was scaring off a particularly nasty boy named Ernie Goad and his gang of friends by catapulting rocks down the hill of their house.

Part III- Welch (Sections 36-43)

As the weather warmed, Little Hobart Street developed a rough sort of charm. One of the best parts of summer was that everyone had time to read. One night in the summer Rex came home terribly beat up. Jeannette was the only one awake and Rex asked her to help sew stitches in his arm. By this point, Rex had taken to disappearing for days at a time. He never offered any explanations, but he sometimes came home with bags of groceries. Food was scarce again, and Jeannette and Brian became expert foragers—finding lunches in dumpsters or stealing corn from local farms. When Jeannette started sixth grade kids made fun of her for being so skinny. Maureen, on the other hand, always had plenty to eat. She had made lots of friends in Welch and had taken to going over to their houses most nights for dinner.

When winter came along that year, things were particularly tough because the house had almost no insulation. The family could not afford coal, but Rose Mary refused to go on welfare like most of the other residents of Little Hobart Street. During the last snowfall of winter, Erma passed away. Rex claimed her liver had given away, but Rose Mary claimed that her drinking was most certainly a form of suicide even if it had taken longer than most suicides do. Rex was distraught over his mother's death, but the kids couldn't bring it within themselves to feel sorry at her loss. After Erma's funeral, Rex disappeared again. When he still hadn't returned after four days Jeannette's mother sent her to find him. Since Jeannette was her father's favorite, she was always the one forced to bring him home. She went from bar to bar until she found her drunken father and brought him back to the house.

Since there was no indoor plumbing in Jeannette's house, the family would go over to Erma's house to take baths once a week. One day while Jeannette was waiting for a bath, her Uncle Stanley tried to molest her and started masturbating next to her on the couch. When Jeannette complained to Rose Mary about it, her mother said that if Jeannette was okay, it was nothing to worry about. To her, sexual assault was a matter of perception. After that day, Jeannette refused to go to Grandpa's for a bath, preferring to wash with whatever small amounts of water she could find at Little Hobart Street.

One day, Jeannette and Brian were exploring in a nearby abandoned house and came across a diamond ring. Excited, they brought their treasure back to their mother. Rather than sell the ring to provide food for the family, Rose Mary kept it as a replacement for her wedding ring, which Rex had pawned years earlier when they needed extra cash. Rose Mary had become more and more moody, suffering from low self-esteem and periods of depression. One day Jeannette suggested that her mother leave her dad. Rose Mary was shocked that Jeannette would even consider such a thing when her father loved her so much. Jeannette said she didn't blame her dad, but the family needed to get away before he pulled everyone down with him. Jeannette's mother refused to consider the option and never told Rex about the conversation.

When summer came around, most kids went to the pool every day. But Jeannette and her siblings were unwelcome there—Ernie and his gang would tease them mercilessly when they showed up. One day Jeannette ran into Dinitia Hewitt who suggested she come to the pool in the morning with her. Although there were no rules about it, it was common knowledge that the black people of Welch swam in the morning while the white people swam in the afternoon. Still, Jeannette went and had the best morning of her life playing with Dinitia in the pool. But she was never invited again and felt uncomfortable going alone. The afternoon of the day Jeannette went to the pool, a man knocked on the door of the house. Jeannette was home alone and didn't let him in but the man said he was from child protection services and had heard there to investigate a case of neglect. He said he would return later to talk with her parents and left his business card. For some reason, the man never did come back, but the experience was enough to convince Rose Mary to clean the house and to get herself a job as a teacher again.

Part III- Welch (Sections 44-53)

That fall Jeannette started seventh grade, which meant she switched to Welch High School. Dinitia Hewitt was at school too, but they never became close friends, somehow understanding that the racial divisions in the town would never allow for such a friendship. The girls did, however, pass notes in study hall. Dinitia had changed over the summer—she seemed more withdrawn and started drinking alcohol during school hours even. She mentioned in her notes to Jeannette something about her mother's boyfriend moving in and the situation not working out well. Dinitia got pregnant and dropped out the next semester. Jeannette saw her around town occasionally, and they always waved but never talked again. Later, Jeannette learned Dinitia had been arrested for stabbing her mother's boyfriend to death.

That year Jeannette started working for the school newspaper, *The Maroon Wave.* The faculty advisor was a woman named Jeanette Bivens, who had been with the school so long she had been Rex's English teacher, as well. Rex had named Jeannette after Miss Bivens because she was the only teacher to ever believe in him. Jeannette worked hard on the paper and decided she wanted to be a journalist when she grew up because it was a profession where what you wrote majorly influenced how people interacted with the world the next day.

At times, Jeannette felt like she was failing her little sister Maureen because she never seriously had anyone to take care of her. Rose Mary hated teaching school and eventually had a meltdown so severe that she refused to show up for her class. Lori pitied their mom because she had to deal with their dad the most. Jeannette disagreed—she blamed her mother for not being able to resist her dad's requests for drinking money and thought that a stronger woman would be able to keep the family from going hungry.

That summer Lori went off to a government sponsored summer program, and Rose Mary went to Charleston to get a teaching certificate. Jeannette was left in charge of the finances but soon discovered it was more difficult than she imagined. When her father asked for money for beer and cigarettes, she couldn't find it within herself to turn him down. Rex also brought Jeannette along to a bar one night so that she would distract the man he was playing pool against. The situation ended badly with Jeannette stuck with the older man upstairs, who was pressuring her for sex. She refused to go out with her dad after that and got a job at a jewelry store to make up the difference from his drinking escapades.

That August when Rose Mary returned she refused to go back to teaching and was unemployed once more. Jeannette told her mom she was just lazy and acting like a child. Rex whipped Jeannette with a belt for disrespecting her mother. After Jeannette swore to herself that she would find a way to leave Welch at some point, she bought a clear plastic piggy bank and began depositing extra money she made from babysitting or doing other kids' homework. She called it her escape fund. Lori meanwhile developed an obsession with New York City after two filmmakers came to Welch. Jeannette told Lori about the escape fund, and they planned to join forces— When Lori graduated high school she would take the money to get settled in New York and then Jeannette would join her later.

By Spring Lori's graduation was nearing, and the kids had raised nearly 75 dollars—Brian had pitched in, as well. But one day Jeannette came home to discover that the piggy bank had been broken, and all of the money was gone. Everyone knew it was Rex who had stolen the money, but he denied it. The kids started saving again, but, by the time Lori's graduation came around, they only had 37 dollars saved up. Luckily, Jeannette arranged for Lori to work as a nanny with a family in their summer home in Iowa. At the end of the summer, the family gave Lori 200 dollars and paid for her bus ticket to New York.

Lori wrote regularly from New York about how surprising it was, and Jeannette decided she didn't want to wait until graduation. She took the bus to join her sister. Rex was hurt by Jeannette's decision to leave and barely spoke to her except for one night when he showed her some blueprints he had made for the Glass Castle. He went on and on about how incredible Jeannette's room would be until she told him he would never build it. When Jeannette left her father gave her his favorite jackknife so she could take care of herself in the big city. Jeannette turned back from the bus and waved at her dad, who just stood there, growing smaller by the second.

Part IV- New York City

When Jeannette reached the City, she moved into a girl's hostel in Greenwich Village with Lori. Lori worked at a German Restaurant, and Jeannette found work at a burger place in Brooklyn. In the middle of the summer, the sisters found an apartment in the South Bronx. The neighborhood wasn't great, but the girls were used to that. Best of all, the apartment had indoor plumbing, and it was all theirs. That fall Lori helped Jeannette find a public school for her senior year in which instead of classes the students signed up for internships all over the city. Jeannette interned for a weekly newspaper in Brooklyn called *The Phoenix*. After she graduated, the editor, Mike Armstrong, offered her a full-time job.

Jeannette wrote long letters to Brian who decided to join her and Lori the following year after his junior year of high school. Mike Armstrong encouraged Jeannette to go to college because, with a degree, she could get a much better journalism job than working at The Phoenix. She applied and was accepted to Barnard College, the women's school associated with Columbia University. She was hired as an editorial assistant at one of the biggest magazines in the city and felt that she had finally made it. Lori decided it was time for Maureen to join the family in New York as well even though she was only twelve. Maureen came over in early winter. She lived with Maureen and enrolled in a decent public school.

Three years after Jeannette had moved to New York City, she was listening to the radio as she got ready for classes and heard a story about a car that broke down on the turnpike. The car's dog got loose, and traffic was stopped for thousands of commuters. That night Jeannette had a phone call from her mother, who announced that she and Rex had moved to New York to be closer to the kids. Jeannette realized that the car on the turnpike had been theirs. Jeannette's parents lived in a boarding house for a while but were evicted when they couldn't pay rent. They moved in with Lori and proceeded to drive her crazy. Rex started sleeping in the car, and Lori eventually kicked Rose Mary out when she refused to get a job and cluttered up the house so much that Lori couldn't stand it any longer.

Rex and Rose Mary started living on the streets. They would call their children regularly from payphones. Rose Mary said being homeless was an adventure. As the weather got colder Jeannette became more worried about her parents. Part of her wanted to help them, but part of her wanted to forget about them. For a while, Jeannette considered dropping out of Barnard to help, but Lori convinced her that getting her degree was still celebrated. Besides, Rex's favorite thing to brag about was that his daughter was a college girl. Plus, as Brian pointed out, their parents did have options. They had land in Texas they could sell, they still owned the property in Phoenix, and they hadn't even tried to get jobs. It seemed to Jeannette that her parents could easily become stable if they wanted it.

Rex and Rose Mary survived the winter, but they looked a little more worn down every time Jeannette saw them. Rex, who almost never got sick, came down with a bad case of tuberculosis and was hospitalized for six weeks. During that time, he sobered up for the first time since Phoenix and after moved to upstate New York where he got a job and seemed to be getting his life back together. However, he moved back to the city when Rose Mary complained that she missed him too much and was soon back to drinking.

By the summer before Jeannette's senior year at
Barnard, her parents had been living on the streets for
nearly three years. Despite their own situation, Rex
still managed to get Jeannette the 2000 dollars she
needed for her final year's tuition by playing poker. A
month later Rose Mary called Jeannette to tell her that
they had found a place to live—they were squatting in
an abandoned building in the Lower East Side.
Jeannette graduated from Barnard that spring and
soon married Eric, a man she had been dating steadily
for three years. Jeannette moved in to Eric's
apartment on Park Avenue, and the two lived a
supremely comfortable life. Jeannette's mother told
her she had sold out.

Maureen meanwhile had graduated from high school
and enrolled in a local college. She soon dropped out
and took on a string of waitress jobs. She switched
from boyfriend to boyfriend, always seeming to be
looking for someone to take care of her. Maureen
moved in with her parents in the Lower East Side but
would fight with them regularly. Jeannette suspected
she was on drugs and tried to get her help. Six months
later, Maureen stabbed Rose Mary in the shoulder
during a fight. She was arrested and sent to a hospital
upstate. At Maureen's arraignment, the whole family
argued over whose fault it was that Maureen had
ended up this way.

After that, Jeannette rarely saw her parents. One day Jeannette's mother called and insisted she come to visit the apartment in the Lower East Side. Her father looked gaunt and told Jeannette he was dying from a tropical disease he had contracted from some Nigerian drug dealers. Jeannette knew this was just another of her dad's stories—although he was only 59, the years of copious alcohol and cigarettes had finally worn his body down. When Jeannette left, Rex winked and asked if he had ever let her down. Two weeks later he died of a heart attack.

Part V- Thanksgiving

A year after Rex died Jeannette left Eric. He was a terrific guy but not the right guy for her. She remarried with a man named John who was also a reporter and also had an intriguing upbringing moving from place to place. Five years after Rex's death, the couple invited the entire family to Thanksgiving in their upstate house—it was the first family get-together since Rex's funeral. Everyone was there except for Maureen, who had moved to California after she got out of the hospital. But Rose Mary said Maureen was even thinking of visiting soon.

Lori was still working as a graphic artist and illustrator in New York. Brian had become a distinguished investigative detective in the NYPD. Rose Mary was as eccentric as ever. As everyone gathered around the Thanksgiving feast, they shared stories about some of Rex's greatest escapades. Rose Mary toasted Rex by saying "life with your father was never boring." It seemed an appropriate tribute.

About BookCaps

We all need refreshers every now and then. Whether you are a student trying to cram for that big final, or someone just trying to understand a book more, BookCaps can help. We are a small, but growing company, and are adding titles every month.

Visit www.bookcaps.com to see more of our books, or contact us with any questions.

46615117R00032

Made in the USA
Middletown, DE
04 August 2017